1960s
FASHION PRINT

A SOURCEBOOK
1960s
FASHION PRINT

marnie fogg

BATSFORD

To my dearest daughter, Emily

First published in the United Kingdom in 2008 by
Batsford
10 Southcombe Street
London
W14 0RA

An imprint of Anova Books Company Ltd

ISBN: 9780713490541

A CIP catalogue record for this book is available from the British Library.

10 9 8 7 6 5 4 3 2 1

Printed by SNP Leefung, China

This book can be ordered direct from the publisher at the website:
www.anovabooks.com, or try your local bookshop.

'Summer of Love' by Natalie Gibson.

Contents

Introduction

Fashion thrives during periods of intense cultural activity. The 1960s saw an explosion of all that was new and modern after the 'make do and mend' of post-war austerity. Against this backdrop of new consumerism, fashion was a persuasive presence in contemporary life, becoming a resounding medium of self-expression. Print was integral to this process, from the Op and Pop Art inspired textiles of the early 1960s to the psychedelic images of the 'Summer of Love'.

Many attitudes and activities thought to characterise the 1960s have their genesis in the previous decade, just as some of them continue into the early 1970s. Mary Quant opened the first trail-blazing boutique, 'Bazaar', on the King's Road in London's Chelsea in 1955, and the fourth and final Biba closed its doors in 1975; between them lay all the print and pattern permutations of an era.

Right: 'Peonies and Carnations' by Natalie Gibson.

Art into Print

The emancipation of the female body from the constraints of 1950s foundations and the tailored complexity of mid-century fashion led to a newly streamlined silhouette. As hemlines rose higher in the mid-1960s, a new proportion evolved in fashion that demanded a fresh print aesthetic. Fussy, small-scale floral designs of traditional fashion fabrics gave way to dramatic large-scale single motifs. At the beginning of the decade these were often appropriated from furnishing fabrics, as the leading contemporary textile designers of the day, such as Barbara Brown and Peter Hall, worked solely on designs for interiors.

The short, sharp little dresses of the early 1960s, simple in design and construction, provided a perfect canvas for the fashion textile designer to showcase creative ideas, many of them influenced by the artistic movements of the period. It was a time when art education required students to pursue innovative design processes alongside practitioners in other fields, resulting in a cross fertilisation of ideas between fashion,

Right: In this design, the dream-like colour harmonies expressed in abstract flowing forms recall the work of several artists, including Russian painter Kandinsky and Swiss artist Paul Klee.

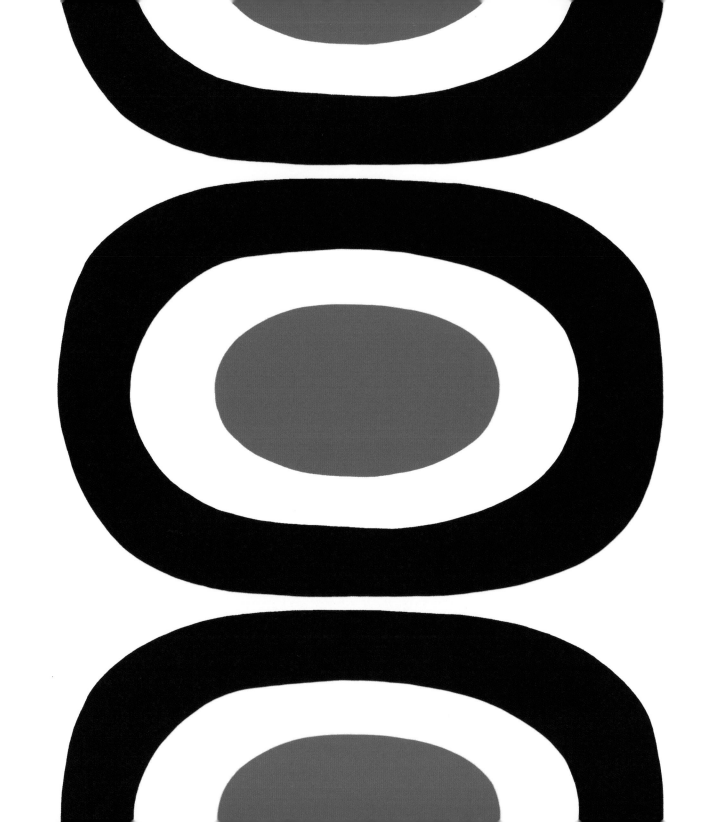

fine art, ceramics, graphics, textiles, and product design. The swirls and splatters of the American Expressionists such as Jackson Pollock that influenced surface and print design in the 1950s were succeeded by Op and Pop Art in the 1960s, providing a fruitful source of imagery for textile designers.

British artist Bridget Riley's first purely optical work *Movement in Squares* appeared in 1961, though the term Op Art was first used by *Time* magazine in 1964 to describe those optical illusions that utilised bizarre perspectives to fool the eye. Larry Aldrich was an American dress manufacturer quick to see the potential of a surface that was so distinctive. He purchased work by both Riley and American abstract painter Richard Anuszkiewicz and commissioned a range of fabrics inspired by his new acquisitions. This trend was picked up by British designer Ossie Clark on his visit to the US with his fellow student David Hockney, and the designer returned enthused about the use of the Op and Pop Art motifs he saw there. His graduation show from London's Royal College of Art in 1964 included an architectural and complex coat of swirling Op Art patterns that was photographed for *Vogue* by David Bailey.

Left: A practising painter as well as designer, Maija Isola was an admirer of the American Abstract Expressionists Mark Rothko, Ellsworth Kelly and Frank Stella. The three concentric circles of the print design 'Melooni' for the Marimekko corporation in Finland are an exercise in pure abstract form on a large scale — the repeat is 97 cm (38 in).

Pop Art had its roots in the late 1950s, named when British artist Richard Hamilton and the critic Lawrence Alloway defined the aesthetic challenge to Europe posed by American industrial culture. According to their manifesto in 1957, the new art should be 'popular, transient, low-cost, mass-produced, young, witty, sexy, gimmicky, glamorous, big business', all tenets that could apply to the print motifs of the era. Pop Art removed the boundaries between high and low culture, elevating mundane imagery and everyday objects such as soup cans, comic books, packaging, magazines and images of celebrities to high art. Consumerism was mediated through the art world in assemblages of cultural icons and found objects, inevitably infiltrating the work of fashion and textile designers.

Targets and flags entered the popular consciousness, referencing American artists such as Jasper Johns, whose range of motifs also included alphabets, and later numerals and maps. He produced his 'flag' painting in 1955, comprised of encaustic, oil and collage on fabric, an assemblage of materials that was to influence all aspects of design in the 1960s. Reproductions of the Union Jack during this era were ubiquitous, appearing on products as diverse as cars, mugs and sunglasses. This was not only as a traditional symbol of patriotism, but also as an image evoking a newly 'Swinging London' as described by *Time* magazine in 1966.

Left and Right and pages 12 and 13: The cartoon-like figures illustrated by Malcolm English in Tom Salter's book *Carnaby Street* (1970), are prompted by the graphic style of the day, also to be found in the Beatles animated feature film *Yellow Submarine* (1968). It was made under the art direction of Heinz Edelmann who pioneered the psychedelic style of the film.

Above: The appropriation of Op Art motifs extends to the shoes in this outfit designed by British designer John Bates in 1965, seen here with model Jean Shrimpton. The collection was destined for an export promotion of British fashion to America aboard the *QE2*.

Right: Fashion, textile and graphic designers deployed the eye-deceiving devices of artists such as Bridget Riley and Victor Vasarely and adapted them to fit a range of ephemeral products. Riley herself threatened a law suit against an American textile designer, fearing that her reputation would suffer by being associated with the transience of fashion.

Left: A scarf designed and manufactured by Swiss textile company Christian Fischbacher, representing the vogue for monochromatic patterning. The print juxtaposes two competing strands in print trends, Op Art and Art Nouveau.

Right: Intriguing and eye-teasing tricks of light and colour are a feature of the shifting and tumbling patterns in this Op Art-inspired design by Liberty of London, produced in 1965.

Left: This design appeared on a short shift dress by dress manufacturer 'California: The Look You Love'. The clashing colours and the loose geometry are resonant of the work of painter Paul Klee.

Right: In the established genre of Op Art, this polychromatic variation creates an excitingly different dynamic to that produced by the more usual black and white.

Left: There is a mixture of Cubist and Pop Art graphic elements in this design, 'Piccadilly Abstract', from the extensive archives of California-based design company Alexander Henry Fabrics. Design directors Phillip and Nicole de Leon, together with their father Marc de Leon, produce two new collections annually and market their fabrics globally. With designs featured in the New York Textile Museum, the company sells to a diverse range of clients, from cutting-edge designers to large corporate manufacturers.

Right: 'All Checked Out' by Alexander Henry Fabrics. This angular composition creates an interplay between the flowing garlands of blossom and fragments of colourful grids, evocative of the geometry of Piet Mondrian's paintings such as *Broadway Boogie Woogie*.

Left: Maija Isola created 533 designs for the Marimekko Corporation in Finland over the course of her 38-year-career. From 1961 she worked for them independently as a freelance designer, and to a significant extent the company is still identified with Isola's aesthetic. The visual directness and clarity typical of her work is evident in the fluidity of this screen-printed pattern, 'Lokki', designed in 1961.

Above and right: British designer Zandra Rhodes graduated from London's Royal College of Art in 1964. The theme behind her diploma show was 'Medals', as seen in this crayon study from her sketchbook (above), and the final eight-colour design printed on cotton sateen (right).

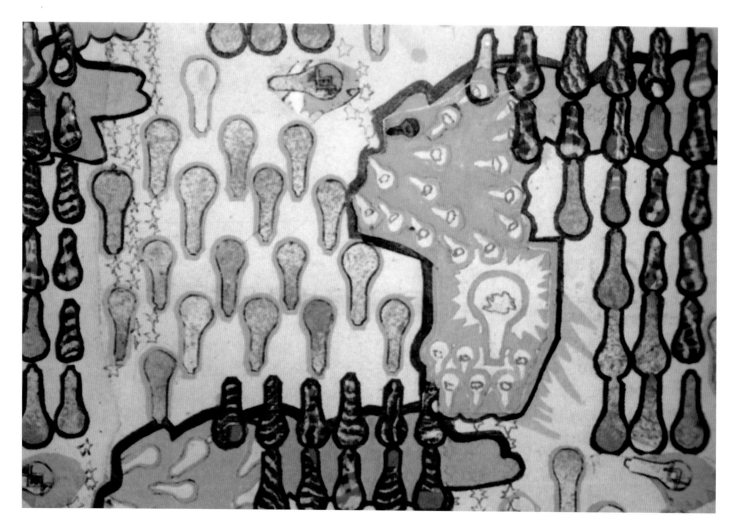

Above, right and overleaf: On graduation, Zandra Rhodes established a print studio with Alexander McIntyre, producing fabrics such as these three versions of her lightbulb design, inspired by the illuminations at British seaside resort Blackpool where millions of coloured bulbs were, and still are fashioned into fantasy extravaganzas.

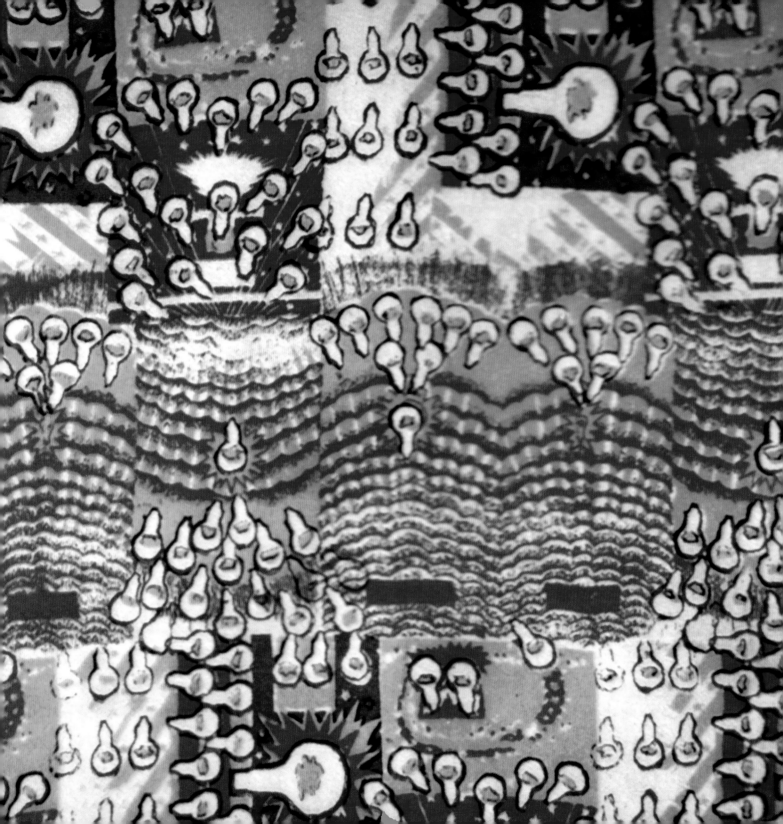

Right: The 'Lipstick' design by Zandra Rhodes was inspired by a Guy Bourdin photograph, typifying the *Pop Art* appropriation of everyday objects as subject matter. A screen was made for each motif and printed separately on to crepe with a repeat of 91cm (36 in). Zandra Rhodes' fabrics were at this time made up in partnership with fashion designer Sylvia Ayton.

Left: A formal arrangement of the repeat heart motif is transformed into voluptuous curves and colours in 'My Love'. It was an award-winning print, designed in 1961 by Natalie Gibson for Danasco Fabrics, founded in 1960. Natalie Gibson is a freelance textile designer who also lectures on printed textiles for fashion at London's Central Saint Martins college of Art and Design.

Above and below right: Behind the exuberant vitality of the colour palette of 'Heaven Sent' by Natalie Gibson, there is a simple, dramatic, geometric repeat. The half-drop repeat in diamond form is infilled with a heart motif in these two colourways.

Left: 'Minab' by Natalie Gibson. A heightened awareness of the impact of colour in all the graphic arts, including textile design, was evident in the adventurous approach to intense and unusual colour combinations. Designer Natalie Gibson approaches the coloration of her designs intuitively, rather than by using colour theory.

Right: Founded in 1951 by visionary textile designer Armi Ratia and her husband Viljo, the Marimekko Corporation in Finland revolutionised the use of the medium of screen printing on an international level. The curvilinear and burgeoning forms of 'Pergola', designed by Maija Isola in 1965, is a design that lends itself to the hand-crafted medium of screen printing. Pattern is at the core of the firm's aesthetic, with substantial cross–fertilisation between fabrics for fashion and those for interior use.

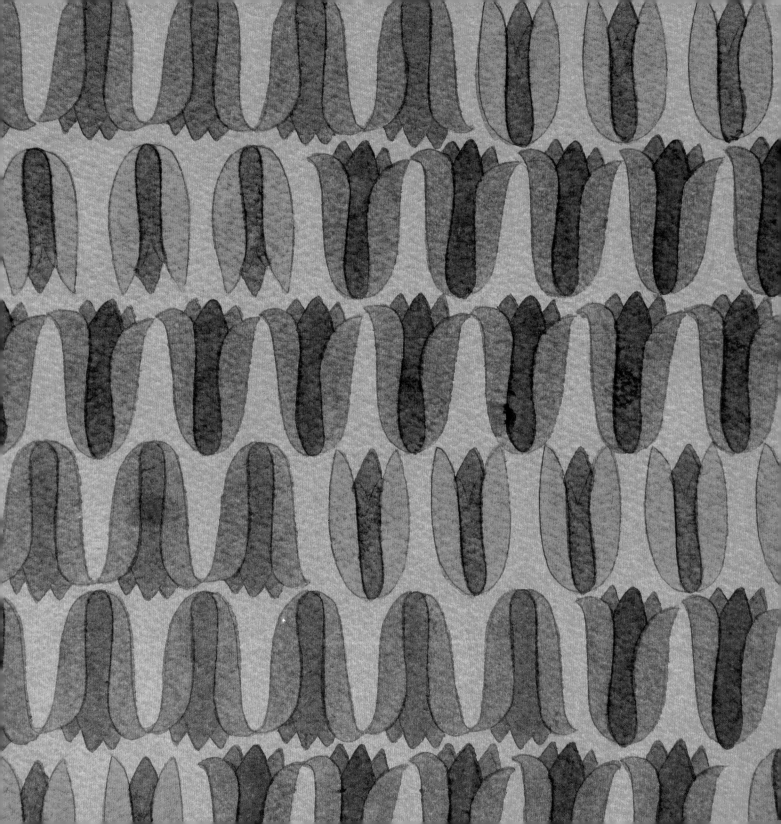

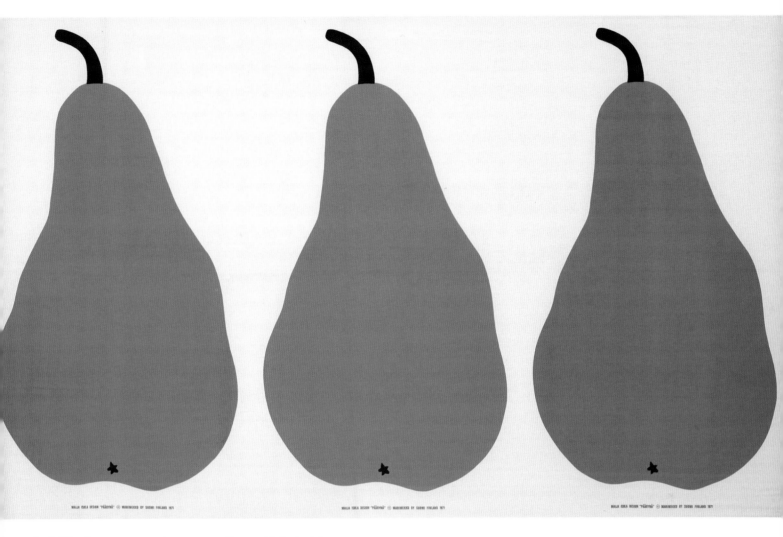

MAIJA ISOLA DESIGN "PÄÄRYNÄ" ⊙ MARIMEKKO OY SUOMI FINLAND 1971   MAIJA ISOLA DESIGN "PÄÄRYNÄ" ⊙ MARIMEKKO OY SUOMI FINLAND 1971   MAIJA ISOLA DESIGN "PÄÄRYNÄ" ⊙ MARIMEKKO OY SUOMI FINLAND 1971

Left: The throw-away simplicity of this design, *'Tulip',* by Alexander Henry Fabrics, belies its subtle variation in the distribution of motifs, generating nuances by use of hand-painted surfaces.

Above: Maija Isola's adventurous approach to scale and composition is evident in this 1969 design for Marimekko, *'Paaryna'.* The simple repetitive pear motif creates an interesting dynamic of positive and negative space.

2 Revivals and Reflections

Pop and Op Art motifs were adopted by the mass-market fashion and textile industry and used by advertisers to sell products from radios to cushions. Designers began to look elsewhere for inspiration. A culture still reeling in shock from the advent of space travel and the new sexual and social mores now embraced nostalgia. Periods of innovation are always followed by retrenchment, and in direct contrast to the hard-edged motifs of modernism and the metallic geometric shapes associated with the space-age, clothes from the past were re-evaluated. Against a backdrop of the new liberalism, the middle of the decade looked back at an era of sexual

Right: American industrial designer Brooks Stevens coined the phrase 'planned obsolescence' in 1954, describing a culture in which the desire for the new replaced the virtues of longevity, as in this 'throw away' dress constructed from bonded cellulose fibre made into paper. The printed pattern shows the move away from the hard-edged geometric designs of modernism into the softer, more fluid lines influenced by the revival of interest in Art Nouveau, while the garment still retains the simple fashion silhouette of the earlier 1960s.

repressiveness and restrictive dress, the 19th century, but subverted the notion of respectability by customising the clothes from the period. Nightdresses and Victorian underwear were worn as outerwear, vintage tea dresses from the 1930s were teamed with Afghan coats, and Edwardian blouses with a minute miniskirt. These were sold in boutiques with names like 'Granny Takes a Trip' and antique markets such as Kensington and Chelsea and London's Portobello Road. The vogue for the past included bygone military uniforms, such as those worn by the Beatles on the Peter Blake cover of their 1967 album *Sergeant Pepper's Lonely Hearts Club Band*.

For print designers, historical revivalism was first invoked through the swirling, free-flowing forms of Art Nouveau, a

term applied to the work of the painters, illustrators and
designers from the late 1890s and the early 1900s. It was a
style characterised by the flowing lines and forms of nature.
Barbara Hulanicki of the iconic boutique Biba
was one of the first designers to recognise the appeal of the
colours and patterns of the 19th-century design visionary
William Morris and the sinuous images of Art Nouveau.
She used a plum and navy Morris print for the curtains in
her Abingdon Road shop in 1964. Hulanicki's aesthetic also
embraced Art Deco and the Hollywood Odeon style with the
opening of the fourth and final Biba in the former Derry &
Toms department store, which had been designed by Bernard
George in 1933 on London's Kensington High Street.

This reappraisal of Art Deco was spearheaded by Bernard
Nevill, Professor of Textiles at the Royal College of Art, and
head of print at London store Liberty. Art Deco began in
Europe in the early years of the 20th century, though it was not
universally popular until the 1925 *Exposition Internationale des
Arts Decoratifs et Industriels Modernes* (International Exposition
of Modern Industrial and Decorative Art). It was influenced
by a variety of sources, from the arts of Africa, Egypt and
Mexico to the streamlined technology and materials of the
'speed age', modern aviation and the rise of the motor car.
These design influences were expressed in the fractional forms
of Cubism and Futurism, and the colour palette of the Fauves.
The influence of the fashion silhouette of the 1930s was also
evident in the longer, more fluid line espoused in the 1960s
by designers such as Ossie Clark. 1967 was the year the film
Bonnie and Clyde was released. Set at the time of the American
Depression, it featured Faye Dunaway and Warren Beatty as
two renegade outlaws, and was enormously influential in
consolidating the growing interest in 1930s fashions and fabrics.

Left: From the Bernard Wardle Company, led by design director Edward Pond from 1962 to 1965, this fabric exemplifies the innovative design and high-quality printing with colourfast vat dyes replacing the chrome dyes of the previous era. Designers of fashion fabrics were not as quick to respond to the trend for large-scale motifs as the designers of home furnishings, causing the flourishing home dressmaking market to appropriate fabrics intended for interiors.

Above: A fabric design from a fashion collection produced by London department store Debenham and Freebody. The traditional design of stylised pineapples and acanthus leaves is rendered here in a vibrant contemporary colourway.

Left: During the 1960s the simple lines of the kaftan, a loose-fitting garment with ethnic overtones, was made popular by the hippie search for unstructured clothing. It was an ideal form with which to express large-scale dramatic prints, as in this wool challis kaftan designed by Jim Thompson for Liberty of London.

Right: Heal Fabrics had a reputation for leading contemporary design, consolidated in the 1960s by the appointment of Design Consultant Tom Worthington, providing a benchmark in design innovation for other companies. This design, 'Rossetti' by Peter Hall, reflects the decade's revival of interest in the works of the Pre-Raphaelite Brotherhood — Dante Gabriel Rossetti was a founder member and an associate of William Morris.

Left: The English propensity for floral prints is given a retrospective quality in this heavily outlined and densely composed design by Bernard Nevill. In an era characterised by freedom of expression, many textile designers retained the precepts of classical composition, for example observing traditional textile repeat formulae.

Left: Liberty of London asked designer Bernard Nevill to create prints that could be used for either dress or furnishing fabrics. The cover of the *Weekend Telegraph Magazine* in 1967 demanded, 'FIND THE LADY. Print on print makes fashion's latest story – and sets a visual puzzle.' This confluence of trends in fashion and interiors is evidenced by Nevill's 'Tango' range of richly coloured, heavily outlined flowers, reflecting the designer's interest in the period between 1913 and 1925. For the first time the home dressmaker had access to the same fabrics as the designer.

Right: From the *Weekend Telegraph Magazine* in 1967: 'Fashion rules still exist – some completely new, some that have never changed – but Op, Pop and Psychedelic Art are destroying one more old diehard: that two patterns should never be mixed.'

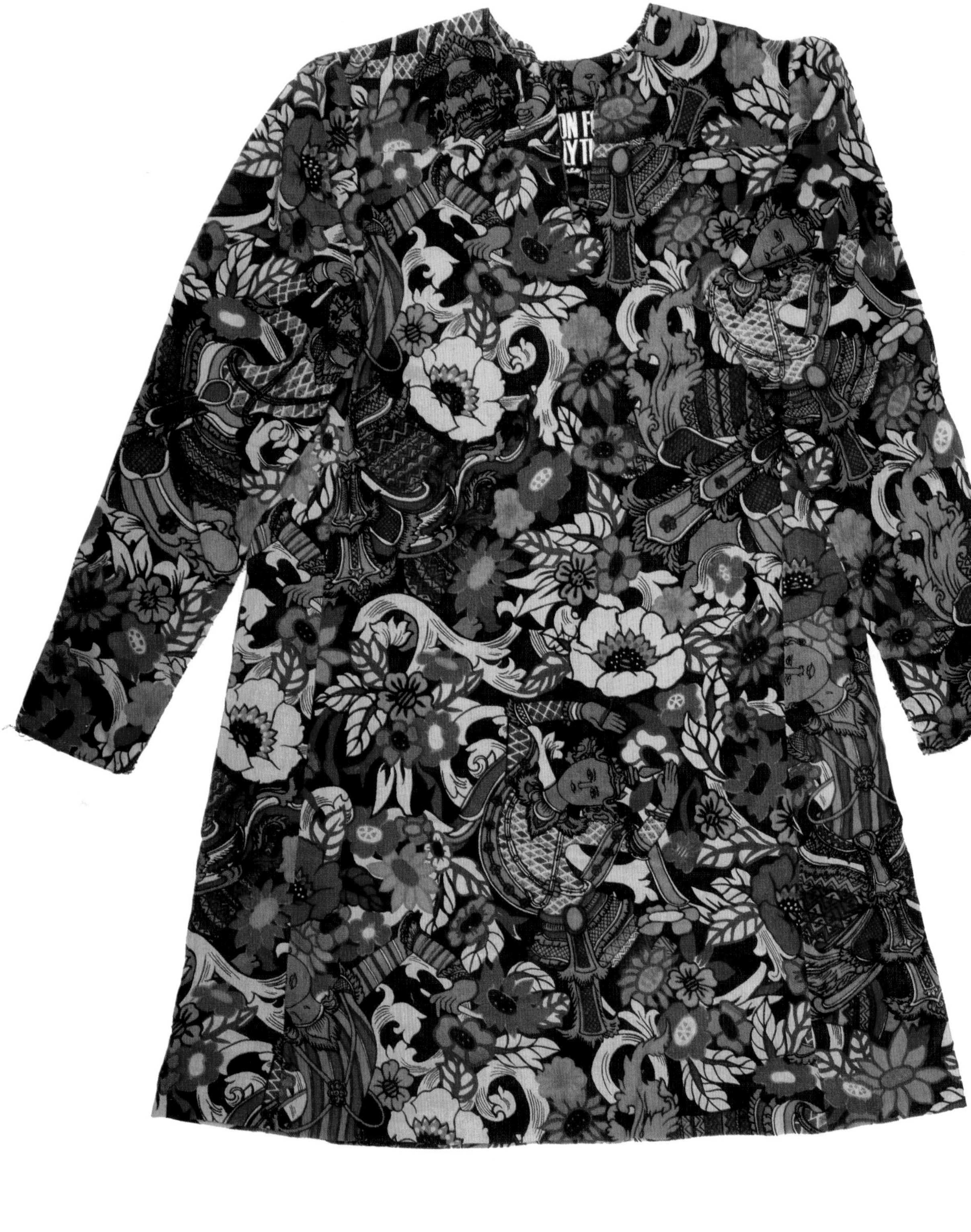

Right: Designed by William Belcher in 1966 for Liberty of London, the stained-glass quality of this print evokes the revival of interest in the *Gothic* style that began early in the 19th century and exercised great influence on taste during the Victorian period.

Left: Textile design by Bernard Nevill for a dress by design label 'Tuffin & Foale'. Marion Foale and Sally Tuffin opened one of the first fashion boutiques in 1962 just off London's Carnaby Street, leading the way in the development of young iconoclastic design.

Left and below: The paisley motif is one of the most enduring inspirations for textile designers. Thought by some to be based on the mark made by impressing the curled inside of the hand onto the cloth, the comma-shaped cone is also recognised as the seed pod, and thus the symbol of life. The motif, though antique in origin, gained popularity with the woven shawls of Kashmir, India, and was imported into Britain at the end of the 17th century. Printed versions soon followed. This 1960s print uses a tight 'flipped' half-drop repeat to produce a balanced interwoven overall effect.

Right: This design was originally introduced in the 1900s and reflected the romantic rural vision of the Arts and Crafts Movement at the end of the 19th century when writers, artists and designers launched a simple back-to-nature ethos. This resonated with the aesthetics of the 1960s, which prompted Liberty of London to reintroduce this design in 1966.

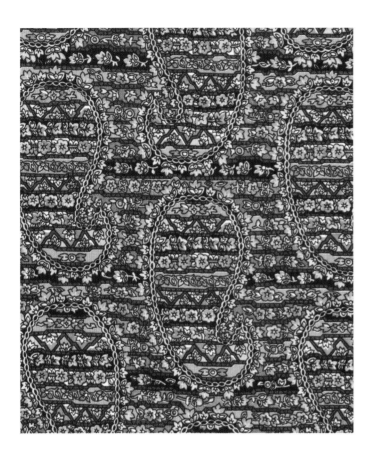

Left and above: The advent of the miniskirt revealed and emphasised the legs. Manufacturers were eager to replace stockings and suspenders with *panty hose, or tights*, providing another opportunity for designers to focus on print. Although 1966 was designated 'the year of the leg', these printed paisley tights were produced in 1964.

Above: The basic scroll-shaped paisley motif is rendered here in a fine lightweight Tana Lawn from Liberty.

Far left: A traditional paisley print in a simple half-drop repeat from a mini dress by fashion label 'Dollyrockers', a title reflecting the trend for describing young women as 'dollies' or 'birds'.

Left: 'Prudence' by Alexander Henry Fabrics intercuts the elaborate stylisation of multi-coloured paisley with more realistic floral elements. The fragmentation of the ground colour creates an impression of layering and perforation, which adds depth to the ornate design.

Right: The extravagantly patterned free-flowing form of the paisley motif was particularly adaptable to psychedelic interpretation, as in this large-scale design in turquoise and purple.

Left: A refreshed traditional paisley design from 1964 produced by London store Liberty, founded in 1875 by Arthur Lasenby Liberty. The store initially imported textiles and object d'art from Asia, and was linked to the aesthetic movement of the 1890s and *Art Nouveau*. Liberty fabrics became one of the foremost proselytisers of the style of that period during the 1960s, resulting in the subsequent popularity of its textile designs.

Right: A complex repeat paisley made fresh with the inclusion of fairground floral elements and vivid colouring. The design has a complex repeat system that maintains a continual flow.

Above: The sinuous lines of *Art Nouveau* are transformed by contemporary coloration and further stylisation in this design. The adipose ogee repeat of this print overlaps into Op Art references with its parallel concentric stripes.

Right: Abstract modular shapes such as these informed much of contemporary design in the 1960s. Here a variant of the ogee repeat form, is made solid with a suggestion of dimensionality through the use of contoured tones. It recalls the *Art Deco* period but also presages the modernist revival of the 1970s.

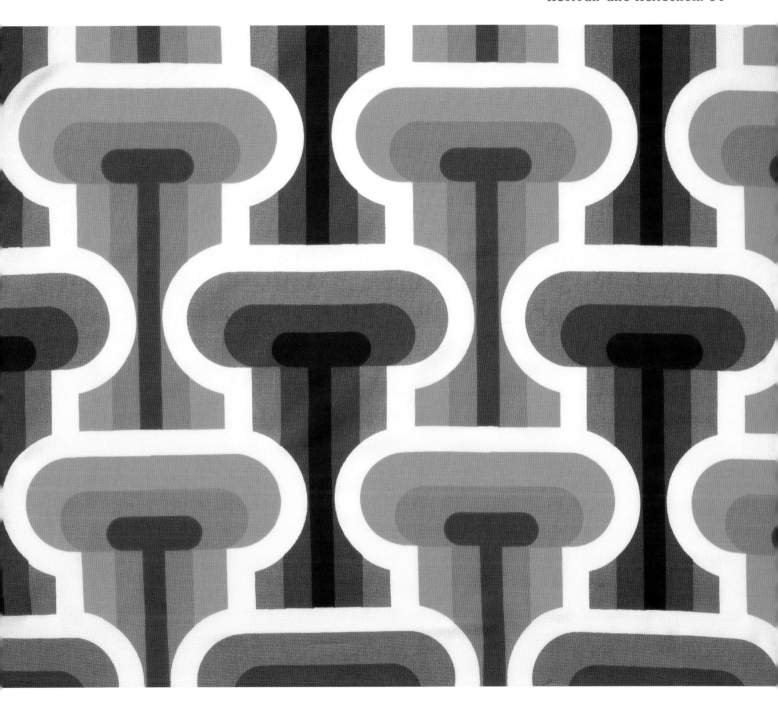

Left and far left:
A similar fluid-edged floral motif is captured in three different ways in these designs by Natalie Gibson. All are superimposed on a rigid grid pattern to create a spatial quality. The subdued neutral background emphasises the playfulness of the motif and the *Art Deco* inspired coloration. Purchased by French company Nicholas Trio, they were used by French fashion designer Emmanuella Khan.

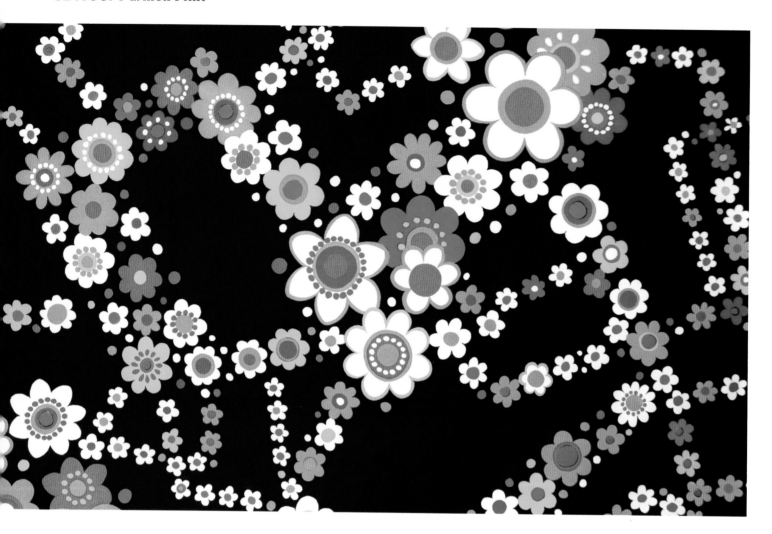

Above: *'Daisy Maze'* by Alexander Henry Fabrics creates an animated surface of multi-coloured daisy chains of various proportions floating above the dark contrast of the background.

Right: Printed on silk, this design of heavily outlined yellow poppies juxtaposes Art Deco stylised blooms with the cartoon-like graphics of the animated film *Yellow Submarine*.

Left: Bernard Nevill (Professor of Textiles at London's Royal College of Art, and head of print at London store Liberty) spearheaded a reappraisal of the Art Deco design movement that infiltrated every aspect of design from furniture to fabric. The dark palette of rich hues recall the seductive contrasts and fragmented vortices of Sonia Delaunay's designs.

Right: Fusing elements of Frank Stella's dimensional painted surfaces, this design, 'Click', by Alexander Henry Fabrics, gains impact from the rhythmic suggestion of space and form reinforced by the acute management of competing colours. The lighter, brighter colour palette roots it firmly in the 1960s.

Above: 'Treetops' by Heal Fabrics. The colour palette of brown and pink anticipates the 1970s trend away from bright pastels and psychedelic hues into a darker, more sultry palette in keeping with the trend for 'Odeon' glamour.

Right: Revisiting the graphic style of 19th-century illustrator Aubrey Beardsley, this is an acutely observed yet highly formalised romantic landscape design by Bernard Nevill.

Left: 'Fantasia' by Natalie
Gibson. The rigid
geometric pattern is
softened by the botanical
references. As with all *Art
Deco* inspired patterns,
natural forms are stylised
into formal structures.

Right: The geometric
fan was one of the most
ubiquitous images exploited
by designers
in the Art Deco period, along
with the sunburst (used for
everything from radiator
grills on cars to
the spire of the Chrysler
Building) and other images
from nature, such as shells
and flowers. This design was
produced in 1966 by Liberty
of London.

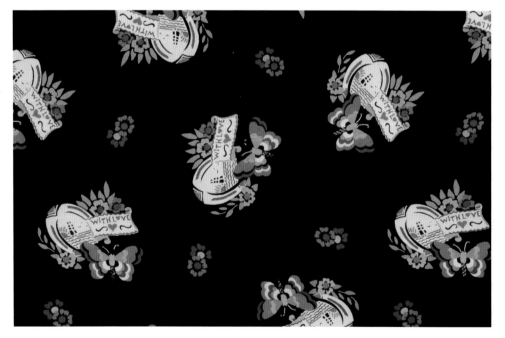

Left, above and below: 'All You Need is Love' by Natalie Gibson is from a range of designs based on tattoos, printed by Italian silk printers Mantero.

Right: Designers find their inspiration from many sources, including travel. This fashion fabric design by Natalie Gibson, used for men's shirting, was inspired by the cut-glass panel in a door of a house in Puerto Rico.

Right: The unrestrained flight of butterflies in this discharge print by Natalie Gibson for British fashion label Stirling Cooper is emphasised by the solid black background. Butterflies were a potent image of freedom in the 1960s. At the Rolling Stones concert in London's Hyde Park, to commemorate the death of guitarist Brian Jones, lead singer Mick Jagger released hundreds of butterflies into the air.

Far Right: Revisiting the 'Odeon' style of the 1930s, when the austerity of Bauhaus modernism gave way to the influence of Hollywood glamour, Bernard Nevill's design depicts a 1930s New York skyline.

Above: The 1930s preoccupation with the exotic –
parrots and hot-house blooms were popular motifs
of the era – influenced this design by Natalie Gibson.

Left: The rectilinear neatness of the horizontal and vertical trellis and the stylised rosebuds at each intersection is contrasted by the seemingly arbitrary placing of the alighting butterfly in 'Nectar', designed for Heal Fabrics by Natalie Gibson.

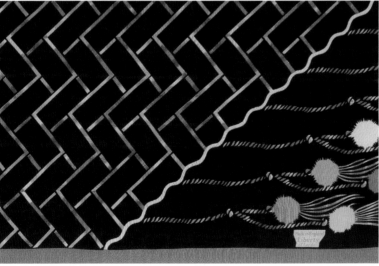

Left: A scarf for the London store Liberty, designed and hand printed by Natalie Gibson, shows a sophisticated replication of an *Ikat* space-dyed effect in the printed stripes and tassels.

Above: Biba was the first fashion boutique to enter the popular consciousness. Opened by Barbara Hulanicki and her husband Steven Fitz-Simon in 1964, they rapidly expanded into larger premises, finally moving the fourth and final Biba into an *Art Deco* department store on London's High Street Kensington. Here the designer offered a total look that reflected the decadence of the *fin de siecle* mediated through the Hollywood glamour of the 1930s. Biba style was epitomised by a plethora of print on both clothes and furnishings. Alexandra Pringle remembers in *The London Look: Fashion from Street to Catwalk* 'At the very beginning Biba was a hang-out for dollybirds...long fringes and large spikey eyes under hats studded with holes like Emmenthal cheese, in shifts made from upholstery fabrics.'

Right: Intimations of two of the most popular motifs from the Art Deco era – the sunrise and the open fan – and the assertive use of strong colour place this design by Natalie Gibson for the American market firmly in the retro mood of the late 1960s.

Illustrations by Malcolm Bird

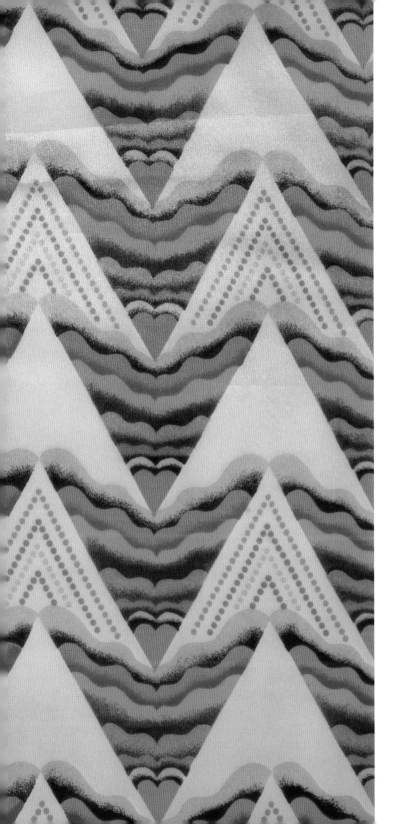

Previous page:
Author and illustrator Malcolm Bird designed these interiors of the boudoir and the bedroom to celebrate the opening of Biba for the windows of New York store *Bloomingdales*.

Left: A cloud-like undulating stripe in this design, *'Up and Down'*, by Natalie Gibson is punctured by a solid pyramid of colour.

3 Flower Power

The counter culture rejected the notion of the mass produced and the machine made. With an aversion to the 'plastic' world, hippies (a word derived from the adjective 'hip' in the spring of 1967), rejected mainstream commercialism. Industrial processes and synthetic products were an anathema to the 'flower children', protagonists in the hippie 'back to nature' life-style. 'Flower Power' symbolised the force of nature against the power of authority, then involved in a long and bloody war in Vietnam. This adherence to an alternative lifestyle outside of mainstream society included a reverence for the homespun and a return to natural fibres. As the hippie subculture moved into idealistic rural communes, fashion became hand-crafted, a forerunner of contemporary concerns with sustainability. The culmination of this desire for free expression came in 1967, the 'Summer of Love', a time of liberation from the perceived constraints of white middle-class suburbia. In the social and political upheavals of 1968, flowers became a potent symbol of peace and love and an expression of a yearning for a pastoral idyll. Even those devoid of the means or resolve to slip off the yoke of conventional employment flagged their sympathies with mildly subversive clothing accessories such as a 'hip' floral tie or vivid headscarf.

Previous page, above and right: A simplified daisy motif in a naive repeat arrangement is bordered by overlapping geometric forms. It was designed by Natalie Gibson for London company Heal Fabrics. With the introduction of new design ranges, the shop assistants customarily wore Heals furnishing fabrics made up into clothes.

Far left: Andy Warhol in his studio with his silk-screen stencils of flowers. Although a departure from his images of popular culture, the flowers are transformed into Technicolor Pop Art blooms.

Left: Designed by Maija Isola during the early era of Flower Power, 'Unikko' remains one of Marimekko's most popular designs. Initially introduced in 1964, the same year as Andy Warhol's cerise and yellow flower paintings, the exaggeratedly flat large-scale poppies are in a repeat of 103 cm (40 ½).

Left and right: The success of these simple designs hinges on the disguised half-drop repeat system. The flattened, stylised daisy motif in a limited colour palette is typical of the early 1960s desire for simplicity and graphic clarity, reducing natural shapes to their simplest forms.

Left: Gingham's image of kitchen curtains and school blouses was left behind when French sex kitten Brigitte Bardot chose the small checked fabric for her wedding dress in 1959. This design of impressionistic gingham by Alexander Henry Fabrics capitalises on the fabrics *ingénue* charm by incorporating it into a daisy design.

Right: '*Sunflower Power*' by Alexander Henry Fabrics harnesses the impressionistic impact of Vincent Van Gogh's treatment of sunflowers in a flowing composition.

Left: Images of flowers, whether stylised, impressionistic or naturalistic, are one of the most enduring sources of inspiration for the textile designer. During the 1960s flowers had a particular resonance with the desire of the counter culture for an alternative lifestyle. 'Flower Power' represented the delights to be had in nature, as opposed to the man-made and the artificial.

Right: A dramatic large-scale discharge print. This is a technique that involves removing colour from the dyed fabric and printing an 'illuminating colour' in the spaces where the ground shade has been 'discharged'.

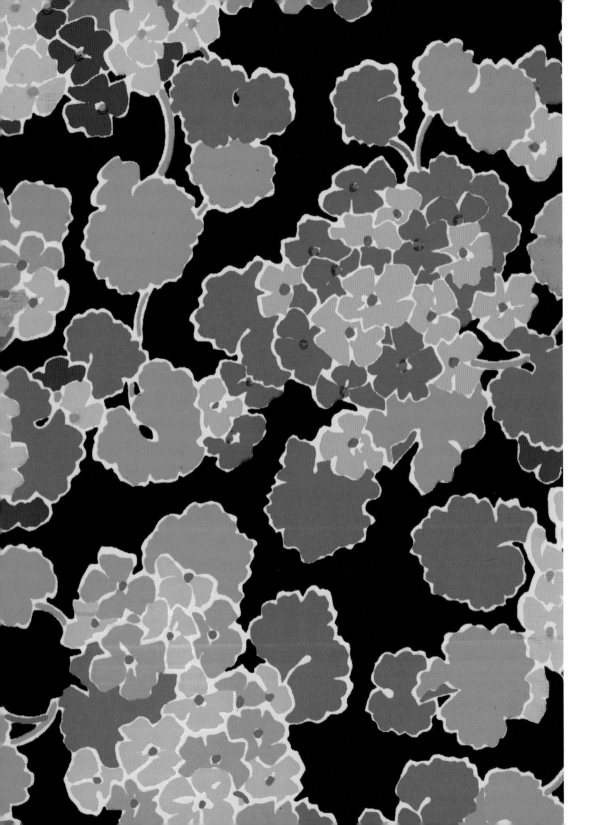

Left: A screen print in which the black background is printed rather than dyed (as is the case with discharge printing). The narrow white outline is a graphic device to lift the flowers from the background.

Right: Simple two-colour screen design on a white waffle cotton ground. This fabric is from Hawaiian label *Malama.*

Above: The prevalence of the daisy motif can be attributed to both the simplicity of its structure – the petals can be formed by one simple brushstroke – and its evocation of innocence.

Right: Flowers have been deployed in an infinite variety of ways by Californian-based design company Alexander Henry Fabrics, as in these exotic Hawaiian blooms in the design 'Waikiki'.

Left: In the design 'Ink Drop Pareo', Alexander Henry Fabrics produces a flowing, garlanded floral repeat on a clear ground. The sense of casual flow is reinforced in the inky outline of the flowers that puddles into the concave intersections of this motif. This was a popular graphic device in many areas of illustration, originating with the use of mapping pens.

Right: 'Judy', by Alexander Henry Fabrics, sets jewel-like fantasy flowers on a dramatic dark ground. The building up of floral patterning within the stylised flowers recalls the millefiori paperweights of Murano glassware.

Left: Traditionally, the soft, fine, floral printed cotton 'Tana Lawn', produced by Liberty of London, was used exclusively for children's wear such as formal smocked dresses and blouses.

Above: Alexander Henry Fabrics use a dark
ground in *'Central Park', shown here* to give
contrast to the formal geometric clusters of
flowers of various scales.

Above: This small-scale sprigged floral half-drop repeat was designed for men's neckties.

Right and far right: In the 1960s designers such as Gerald McCann and Marion Foale of Tuffin & Foale appropriated Tana Lawn for the 'dolly bird' dresses of the era, depicted here by the renowned fashion illustrator Bobby Hillson.

Previous page, above and above left: Designs for Tana Lawn by Liberty of London.

Right: Floral designs during this period rarely recorded a structural, botanical view of plant motifs. The undulating stems culminating in extravagant many-petalled blooms render this design by Liberty of London in 1966 purely decorative.

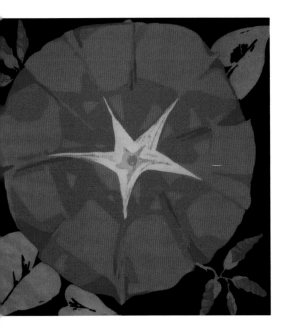

Above: When the American designer Ken
Scott arrived in Italy in 1955 he embarked
on the production of printed fabrics that
featured exuberant design and lavish
coloration. Gigantic, exotically hued florals
such as this design of a convolvulus in 8
colours, 'Cinque e Mezzo', advanced his
success as a design pioneer in the
following decades. This image is from the
Ken Scott Archive, Milan.

Left: Originally a painter, Ken Scott became known as the 'fashion gardener' for his complex rendition of flowers, such as this design 'Vrai Papa', a portrait of poppies in 15 colours in a square repeat. This image is from the Ken Scott Archive, Milan.

Below: A 12-colour non-repeating design, 'Ilan', by Ken Scott. To generate a realistic depth of field this print exploits the impact of a dense mass of irises with foliage of receding tones. This image is from the Ken Scott Archive, Milan.

Above: 'Lizzie', an 8-colour half-drop repeat by Ken Scott, is an aerial impression of Nigella Damascena or 'love-in-a-mist', which unusually uses the white ground of the fabric to provide the backdrop to the silhouetted network of the flower's characteristically haphazard foliage. This image is from the Ken Scott Archive, Milan.

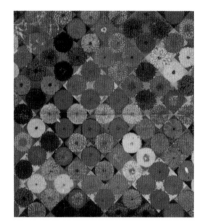

Above: 'Jandan', a half-drop repeat design, in 14 vibrant colours, from the Ken Scott label. The designer has superimposed his ebullient portraits of flower heads – in this case chrysanthemums – upon a rigid diagonal geometric ground. This image is from the Ken Scott Archive, Milan.

Right: In this design, 'Luluzi', by Ken Scott, the explosive cornucopia of dahlia blooms recognises the influence of psychedelic saturation of colour. This image is from the Ken Scott Archive, Milan.

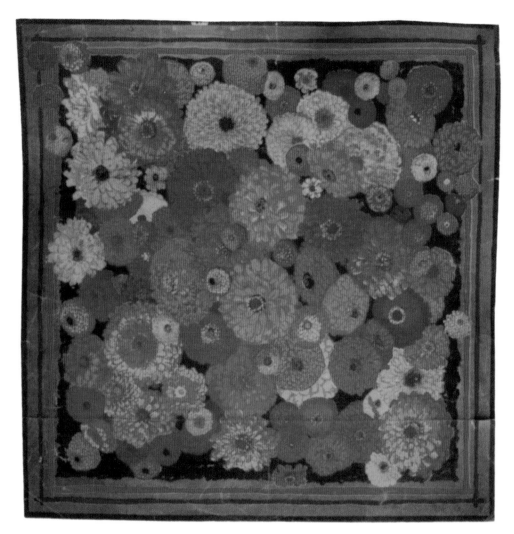

Left: A painterly evocation of a posy of marguerites on a verdant green ground, this design, 'Ghita', was designed in 1967 by Ken Scott as a silk scarf. This image is from the Ken Scott Archive, Milan.

Right: The counter culture infiltrates couture.
This complex all-over print appeared on a
gown by British couturier Hardy Amies.

Left: 'Shinjuku' is a two-colour fabric by Alexander Henry Fabrics. The colour choice of red, black and white and the subject of chrysanthemums makes a direct connection to the influence of the style of Japanese print design.

Above: The animation of the motifs in this discharge-print design, 'Odette', by Alexander Henry Fabrics, epitomises the ability of the drawn line to portray spontaneity and vivacity of expression.

Left: Carnations and peonies are rendered in the style of Chinese stencils on a powdered ground in this design by Natalie Gibson.

4 'Lost in Multicoloured Hues'

The all-pervasive, mind-expanding hallucinogenic drugs available in the 1960s heightened and distorted perception, resulting in kaleidoscopic colours and mesmerising patterns. Leading advocate of LSD, Harvard professor, Dr Timothy Leary, named the drug in 1966 *Playboy* magazine as 'the most potent hallucinogenic drug known to science'. Hippie culture, with its origins in the American Beat movement, embraced LSD or 'acid' as the drug of choice, and gave it names such as orange sunshine, blue light, purple haze and blue cheer. Even the acid tabs were decorated with psychedelic imagery. Light shows replicated the hallucinogenic experience; a mix of water and coloured oils on top of an overhead projector vibrated to the music, projecting liquid colour images onto moving, naked bodies to create living patterns.

Right: In 'Sunshine of Your Love' hearts, flowers and vivid colours – all part of the iconography of the 1960s – are drawn together in this flowing stripe design by Natalie Gibson. It epitomises the playful insouciance of the era.

The drug culture iconography entered print design, pattern became personal, and adornment encompassed the human form and its environment. Exotic ornamentation embellished and decorated surfaces, including the naked body, clothes, cars, interiors, album sleeves, even the facades of buildings. The exterior walls of boutiques such as The Fool, run by Dutch-born Marijke Koger and financed by the Beatles, were decorated from ground to roof with the same psychedelic imagery and juxtaposition of pattern as the clothes inside.

A confluence of images, from such diverse sources as the work of 19th-century British artist Aubrey Beardsley (exhibited in London's Victoria and Albert Museum in 1966) and the poster art of Alphons Mucha, inspired the graphic style of the 1960s counter-culture artists. It included Nigel Waymouth and Michael English who worked under the name of 'Hapshash and the Coloured Coat'. The densely patterned and graphic complexity of the rock poster influenced mainstream commercial art, including textile design. The underground movement became the first subculture to fuse fashion, music and the graphic arts, resulting in a convergence of trends that infiltrated every aspect of the designed object, including print design for fashion and interiors. As Richard Neville wrote in his book *Playpower*, published in 1970, 'An ingredient common to hippie street demos, altered consciousness, Dylan's lyrics, group sex and the Underground arts/media scene was playfulness.' This is evident in the subject matter of the fashion prints of the era: hearts and flowers, fantasy landscapes, balloons and butterflies and the influence of animated cartoons such as *Yellow Submarine*.

This extravagant and multi-patterned excess extended from the counter culture into high-status fashion. Although his aesthetic was the antithesis of formal haute couture, legendary Italian designer Emilio Pucci's distinctive abstract swirls of acid-bright colours were synonymous with the new jet-age. Inspired by his own travels to exotic locations such as Bali, Indonesia, Africa and South America, and mixing in his own Italian heritage of Renaissance paintings and the Pallio race, Pucci mediated these influences through a complex fusion of colours. Labelled the 'Prince of Prints' by the American press, his singular palette encompassed vivid combinations rarely seen before: fuchsia and geranium, sapphire and blackberry, khaki and lavender, cardinal red and sea-blue.

Below: 'Take a Trip' By Alexander Henry Fabrics.

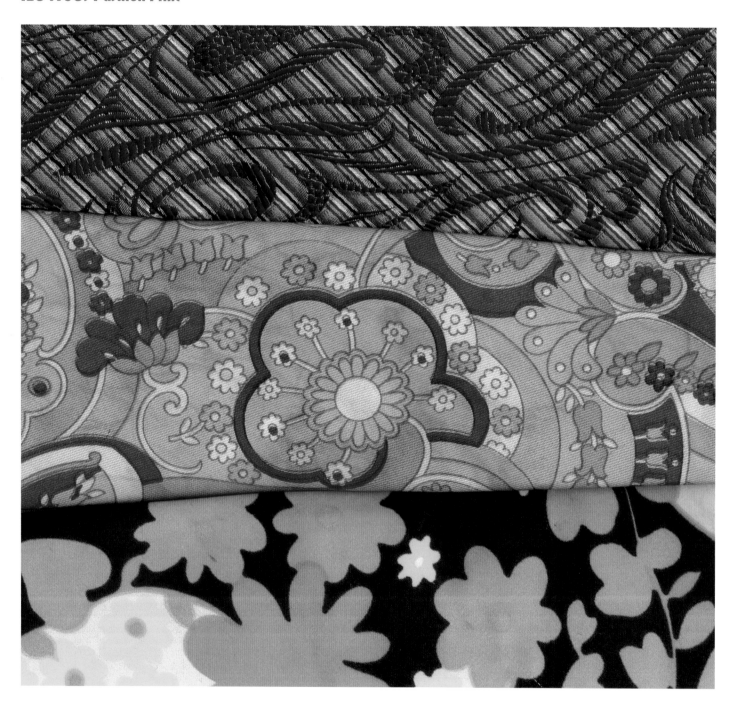

Left: 'Flower Power' even extended to that most conservative item of male clothing, the necktie. It was an acceptable way for even the most establishment figure to participate in the patterns and colours of the counter culture.

Above: A six-colour print from three screens, 'The Summer of Love' was designed and screen printed by Natalie Gibson.

Left: Designed for Conran by Natalie Gibson in 1967, 'Shimmy' was described as follows: 'shaking swirls of colour, loud but not deafening get your eye in for an eyeful of four amazing colourways.' This was the first of her designs for British designer and manufacturer Terence Conran.

Above: Two colourways of a design by Natalie Gibson, displaying the light-hearted quality inherent in typical 1960s print design. In an era when a generation had a different outlook on the virtue of traditional working patterns, it was inevitable that the clothes and culture surrounding them would reflect the inherent playfulness of a youth-obsessed culture.

Right: In 1966 Twiggy (Lesley Hornby) had her seminal haircut by Leonard and became the face of the decade. Here, she wears a waistcoat and trousers designed by Natalie Gibson, the pattern carefully placed to optimise its impact. She stands alongside a display mannequin of her face and form by Adele Rootstein.

Far right: This design, hand-screen printed by the designer Natalie Gibson, is an example of a three-colour screen print — yellow, pink and turquoise — producing six colours. Yellow and pink = orange; turquoise and pink = mauve; and yellow and turquoise = bright green.

Left top and bottom: Two colourways of 'Far and Away', designed by Natalie Gibson. The title implies that the pattern-filled circles are balloons, a popular symbol of lightness and freedom, because they can float away without restraint into the distance.

Right: Baubles and bubbles, animated by their different patterning, in this design, 'Tamara', by Alexander Henry Fabrics.

Left: Reveries of a bygone fantasy childhood where trees sprout flowers and the sky is pink, are suggested by this dreamscape, 'Tree of Life', by Alexander Henry Fabrics.

Right: Laurel Canyon meets Alice in Wonderland in this design by Alexander Henry Fabrics. The trend for imaginary landscapes was in part influenced by the animated cartoons of the day, but also reflects the interest in children's fantasy fiction, which was popular at the time.

Left: 'Spinning Wheels' by Alexander Henry Fabrics. The peacock is a bird of mythical status, a potent signifier of excessive display, and thus perfectly in keeping with the flamboyance inherent in the fashionable dress of both men and women in the free-thinking 1960s.

Right: In this design, 'Gemma' by Alexander Henry Fabrics, the 'posterisation' of these floral forms recalls the poster art of Toulouse Lautrec, which in turn inspired the rock poster genre of the period.

Left: A fantasy landscape design by Alexander Henry Fabrics that defies reality in both scale and coloration.

Right: 'Sir Peter Peacock' by Alexander Henry Fabrics. Peacock feathers have always been associated with a certain decadence, from the Aesthetic Movement of the late 19th century to the Art Nouveau revival in the psychedelic 1960s, a period renowned for licentiousness and sexual display.

Above: In the 1960s Italian designer Emilio Pucci, the 'Prince of Prints', designed for the newly mobile 'beautiful people', style setters and celebrated 'jet-age' beauties such as Jackie Kennedy and Audrey Hepburn. His signature style was abstract non-figurative form in psychedelic swirls of dazzling colour, and his clothes were one of the most enduring status symbols of the 1960s.

Left: Pucci meets the *Yellow Submarine* in this vivid dress print with its contorted imagery and fiery colours.

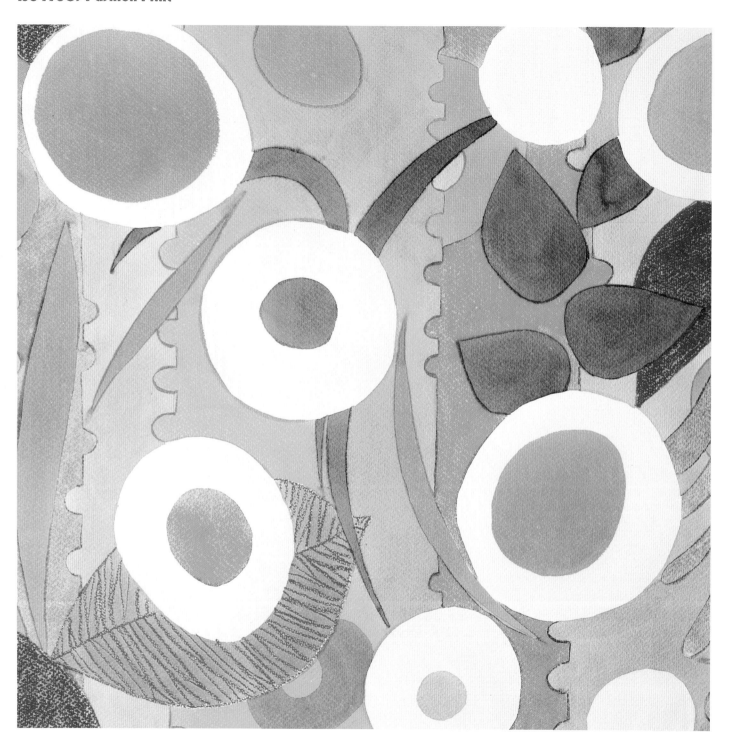

Left: A variety of forms, some abstract, some of tenuous reality, float in a series of layers and cleverly related colours in this design by Alexander Henry Fabrics.

Above: A fusion of fairground patterning with fragmented concentric oval forms gives a strong disjointed geometry to this Alexander Henry Fabrics design 'Zig Zag Abstract'. The bright palette is anchored by the graphic rigour of the black components, suggesting overall the frivolity of a cascade of patterned glass walking sticks.

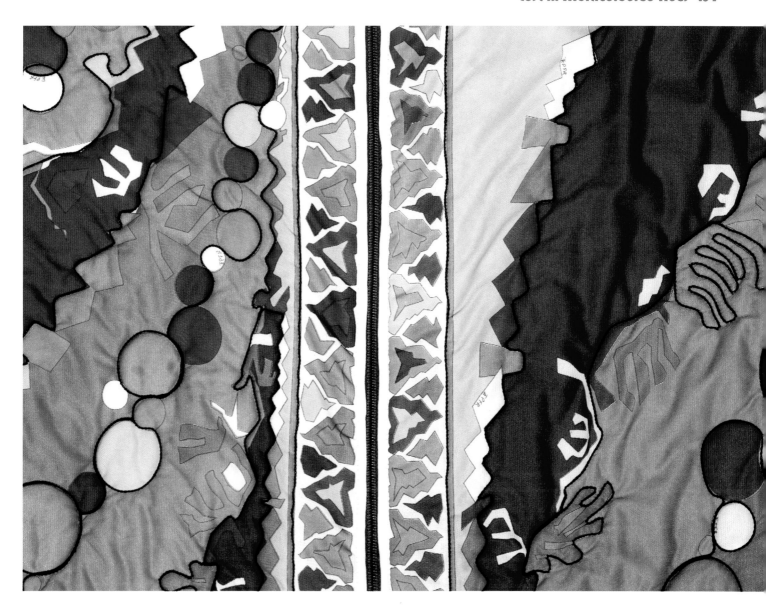

Left: The signature swirling psychedelic patterning of Italian label Pucci was easy to replicate. This convincing rendition of Pucci style was a mass-market label treatment of voided paisleys and fantasy flowers.

Above: A quilted fabric for an après-ski skirt from Italian design label Pucci, showing the typical way in which the designer used borders to contain the free-flowing form of the pattern.

Above and right: One of
the collection of fabrics
designed by Natalie Gibson
for British designer and
entrepreneur Terence
Conran.

Far right: Psychedelic
surges of colour in 'Marvy'
by Alexander Henry
Fabrics.

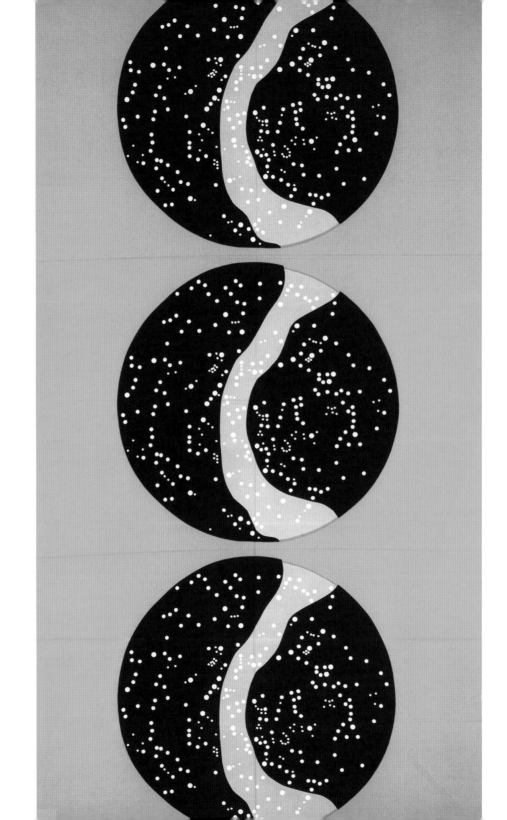

Left: 'Linnunrata', designed by Maija Isola for Marimekko, was inspired by the Apollo moon landing in 1969. The motifs take up the full width of the fabric.

Above: As the necktie was for men, accessories were a way for the conservatively dressed woman to acknowledge current trends, as in this scarf by French design house Yves Saint Laurent. This design demonstrates a formula that is often used in balancing colours: two tones plus two tones plus a contrast colour.

Right: A liberated and enlarged paisley derivative in contrasting colours by Jacqmar.

Above and left: The convoluted spatial framework of this design has an energetic impact. The restless movement of form, colour and pattern infill gives a fitting animation to this cartoon-like composition.

Left and above: This mass-market dress fabric represents the way in which 'consensus' design uses the common denominators of separate avant-garde movements to create an acceptable distillation of trends.

Right: In this Tana Lawn design, the Liberty print comes close to connections with psychedelia but with a Gothic Revival resonance.

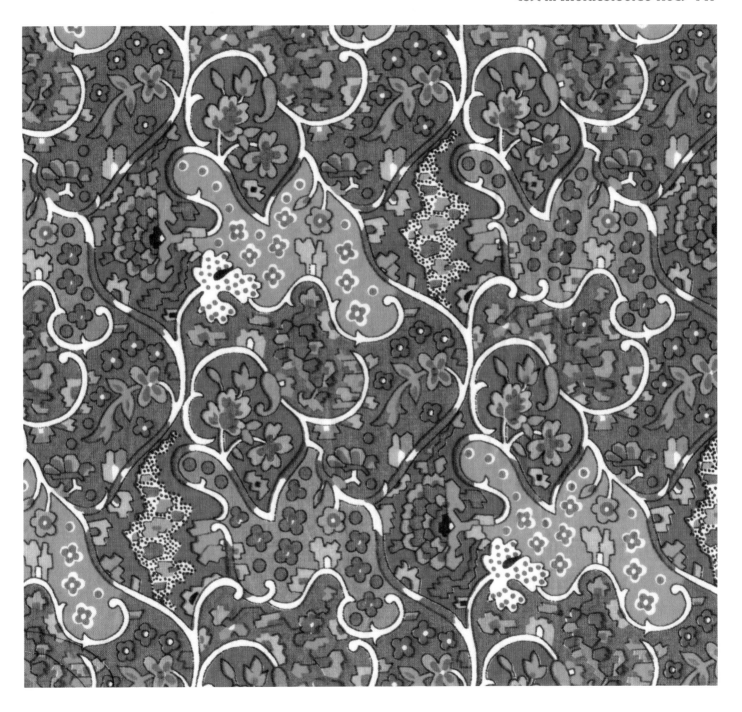

Above: A scarf designed and printed by Natalie Gibson using only one screen. The extra butterfly motifs reflecting the 1960s interest in Orientalism are hand painted.

Right: The effect of hallucinogenic drugs on visual perception was to heighten and distort both colour and pattern. Such imagery influenced all aspects of design, including fashion prints, as in this design of exaggerated butterfly wings 'On the Wing' from the archive of Alexander Henry Fabrics.

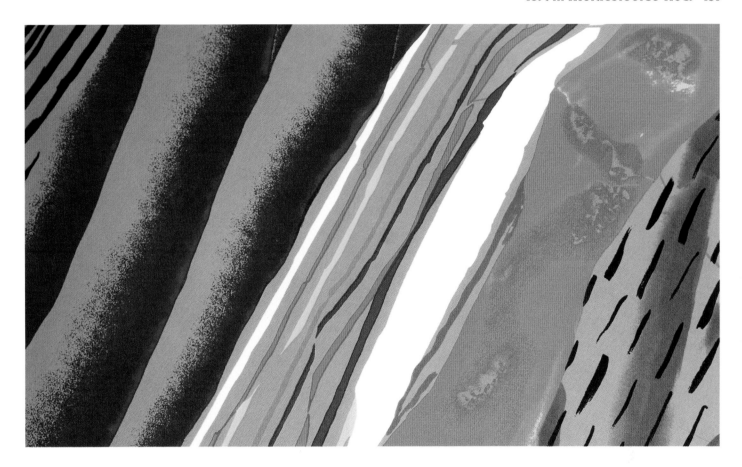

Left: 'Take a Trip' from the Alexander Henry Fabrics archive references the terminology of hippie culture when *tripping* was a hallucinogenic activity rather than a physical journey. This design exploits the marvels of rainbow hues in a swirl of colour.

Above and right: Painterly marks of broken colour and saturated stripes are printed on silk chiffon in this design by Bernard Nevill.

Above and right: 'Chrysalis' (above) and
'Monarch' (right) by Alexander Henry Fabrics
utilise the iridescent and magical patterning
found in the marvels of the natural world.

Left: Wavy lines and disjointed pattern
combine on this seascape, 'Float Away',
by Natalie Gibson.

5 Magical Mystery Tour

The desire for self expression inherent in the burgeoning hippie culture included producing textile designs with techniques picked up on global travels such as batik, tie-dye, two-tone *ombre* and indigo prints. Such images prompted recognition by print designers of the appeal of the exotic and reverence for the rare. The sexes looked indistinguishable as the counter culture pushed the boundaries of gender roles to their limit. Patterns, colours and textures were worn irrespective of gender.

As the decade progressed into the 1970,s an eclectic appropriation of other cultures was fuelled by a generation on the hippie trail to India and the Far East. Multicultural explorations of print designers such as Zandra Rhodes, Natalie Gibson and Celia Birtwell reflected the wanderlust inherent in the era of the hippie.

Right: By cross fertilisation of the folk textile traditions of batik and paisley, this design, 'Batik Paisley Dot', by Alexander Henry Fabrics, gives a fresh rendering of both conventions in one bright print.

Left: This Alexander
Henry Fabrics design,
'Jaipur Paisley', makes
direct reference to the
geographical origins of
the composition.

Right: *'Darjeeling'* by
Alexander Henry Fabrics
combines the enhanced
reality of vibrant colour
and fine detailing redolent
of spice markets with
the intricacies of
temple carvings.

Left: With its saffron shades and a rhythmic bordered pattern, this design is redolent of the Middle Eastern mandala and suggests the aesthetic of the Indian sub-continent. Print design began to reflect the popularity of the 'hippie trail' as a generation trekked to India, Morocco and the Far East in search of an alternative way of life.

Right: The radial symmetry of this highly detailed fabric design manages to reference a panoply of symbols associated with the search for spiritual enlightenment. It has the psychedelic kaleidoscopic imagery, and the patterned delicacy and vibrant colour of Eastern textiles.

Left: The appeal of this one-colour, single-screen design by Natalie Gibson lies in the patchwork arrangement of patterned squares.

Right: Print design 'Granny' by Natalie Gibson is a facsimile patchwork for British textile company 'Hull Traders' whose fabrics were marketed under the name *Time Present*. Under the auspices of design and colour consultant Shirley Craven, the company were committed to a contemporary aesthetic and the fabrics hand screen-printed using mainly pigment dyes. This design reflects the late 1960s burgeoning enthusiasm for the hand crafted when artisanal skills became re-evaluated in the counter-cultural desire for a sustainable lifestyle.

Calumet — Dakota.

Far left and above: A visit to the National Museum of the American Indian in New York City inspired designer Zandra Rhodes' interest in Native American culture. These drawings from her sketchbook show the preparatory stages in processing an idea from primary research into the final cloth and garment of the designer's *Indian Feather* collection.

Left: Four-colour *Indian Feather border print on silk chiffon by Zandra Rhodes.*

British designer Zandra Rhodes set up her first print studio with fellow student Alex MacIntyre on leaving London's Royal College of Art in 1964. Initially drawing on Pop Art motifs and comic-book images to sell to fellow fashion designers such as 'Tuffin & Foale', Rhodes then became preoccupied with developing the print in conjunction with the garment to produce a cohesive whole. Consulting *Costume Patterns and Designs* by Max Tilke, the designer referenced the desire for the folkloric then permeating fashion culture. Her sources included the art and artefacts of other cultures, Chinese fretwork, the beadwork and feathers of the Native American, and images from the Australian outback.

Left, top and bottom: Further drawings from the designer's sketchbook inspired by the National Museum of the American Indian. Primary research is one of the most important tools of the designer, animating and inspiring the creative direction of each collection.

Right: An all-over print showing the final resolution with Native American imagery.

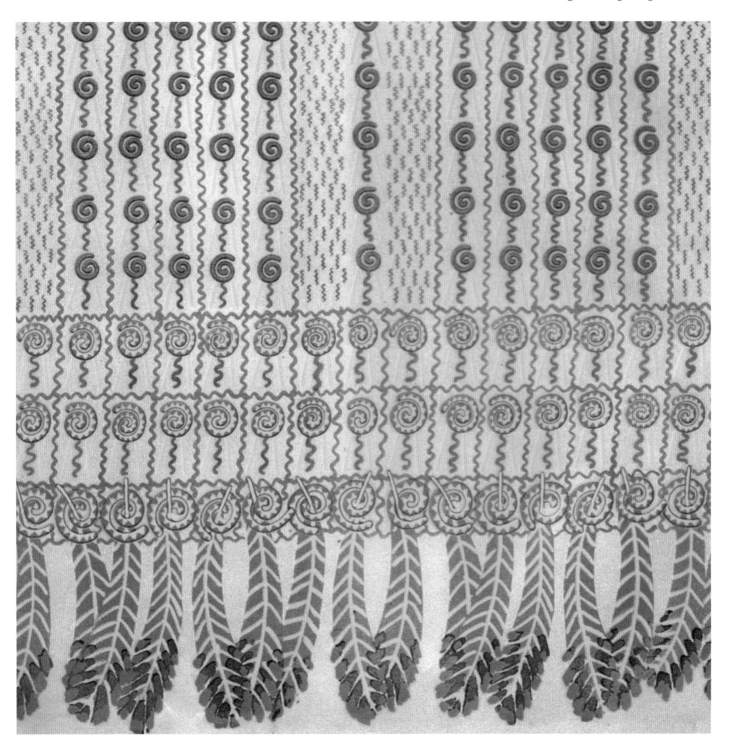

Right: Short kaftan in silk chiffon printed in cobalt, ginger and turquoise in '*Indian Feather Sunspray*'. The edges of this square-cut shape are cut along the lines of the print and hand rolled.

Far right: Kaftan in '*Indian Feather Border*' print on red silk chiffon. Separate strips of 'feather border' hang from the ruched yoke with sleeves gathered horizontally and trimmed with velvet ribbon.

Left: Victorian 'Piano' tasselled shawls were ubiquitous in the 1960s. Found in charity shops and second-hand stores, they were worn over jeans and dresses, or even wrapped around the body. Zandra Rhodes juxtaposed the embroidery and tassels of the shawls with folkloric flowers, resulting in the *'Chevron Shawl'* collection, printed on unbleached calico.

Right: Waistcoat in *'Chevron Shawl'* print in cream silk with quilted yoke. The 'V' shape of the body is formed by the edge of the print, and the tasselled fringe is emphasised by the addition of brown cock feathers.

Left: Coat in 'Chevron Shawl' print. The print is inspired by a stylised fringe shawl on unbleached calico. The edges of the fringe are cut out and stitched around to show the print on either side. The calico is bagged out and quilted.

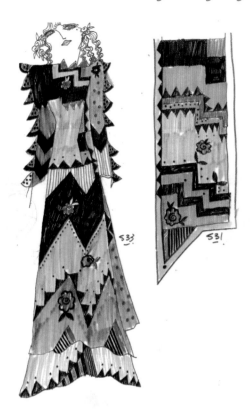

533   531

Celia Birtwell designed prints that were engineered around the subtle architecture of fabric cut with an exquisite sensitivity to the body. Her partnership with fashion designer Ossie Clark resulted in the perfect synthesis of print and garment. The fluid sophistication of Clark's pattern cutting, redolent of the 1930s flowing lines and bias-cut technique exemplified by couturier Madame Vionnet, enhanced the impact of the highly refined and complex layering of print by Birtwell. Her complex and sophisticated designs were printed under the aegis of Ellen Haas at Ivo Prints in Southall. One of the designer's major influences at the time was the Sotheby's auction in 1967 of vintage costumes designed by Leon Bakst for the *Ballet Russes*.

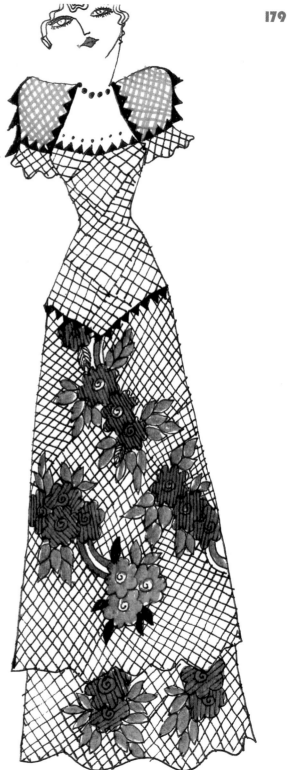

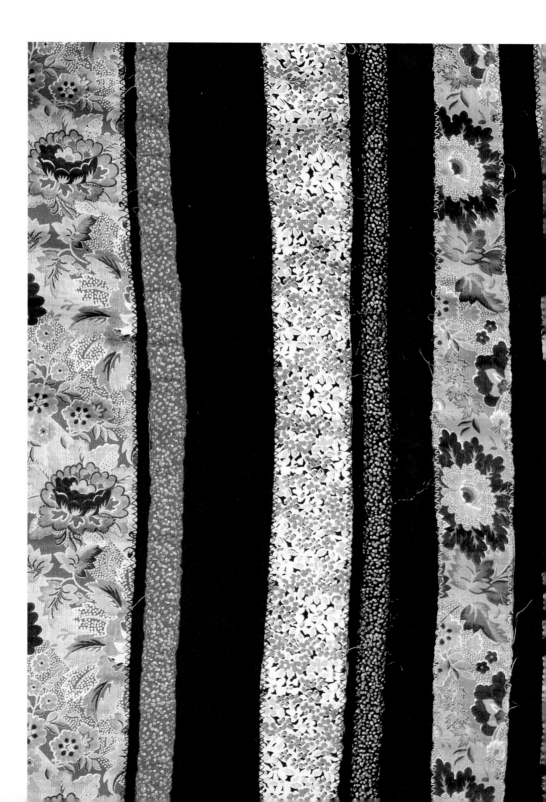

Right: Patchwork expressed the counter culture's eagerness to recycle, seen here in Bernard Nevill's floral striped patchwork for the Italian company Cantini.

Left and far right: Folkloric appliqué top and matching all-over print. This is a luminous design of simplified flower forms grouped into startlingly coloured bouquets by Bernard Nevill for Italian cotton manufacturer *Cantini*. The passionate use of exotic colour combinations is redolent of the decorative traditions of other countries.

Right: In this complex composition
Bernard Nevill takes a cocktail of existing
decorated artefacts and renders them in a
fluid design, rich in colours, reflecting the
diversity of cultural sources. The resultant
design, produced for *Cantini,* is both exotic
and flamboyant.

Bibliography

Aav, Marianne, (ed) *Marimekko, Fabrics, Fashion, Architecture*. Catalogue published in conjunction with the exhibition Marimekko: Fabrics, Fashion, Architecture held at the Bard Graduate Centre for Studies in the Decorative Arts, New York Yale University Press,
New Haven and London.

Bender, Marylin, *The Beautiful People*. Coward McCann New York, 1967.

Breward, Christopher; Ehrman, Edwina; Evans, Caroline. *The London Look: Fashion from Street to Catwalk*. Yale University Press. New Haven & London in association with the Museum of London 2004.

Fogg, Marnie. *Boutique: a 60s Cultural Phenomenon*. Mitchell Beazley 2003.

Hulanicki, Barbara. *From A to Biba*. Hutchinson 1983.

Jackson, Leslie, *20th Century Pattern Design, Textile & Wallpaper Pioneers*. Mitchell Beazley, London 2002.

Kennedy, Shirley, Pucci: *A Renaissance in Fashion*. Abbeville. New York 1991.

Lobenthal, Joel, *Radical Rags*. Abbeville 1990.

Marwick, Arthur, *The Sixties*. Oxford University Press 1998.

Neville, Richard. *Hippie hippie shake*. Bloomsbury Press, London 1995.

Rhodes, Zandra with Knight, Anne. *The Art of Zandra Rhodes,* Cape, London 1984 and Houghton Mifflin, Boston 1985.

Rhodes, Zandra. *A Lifelong Love Affair with Textiles*. Antique Collectors Club Ltd and Zandra Rhodes Publications Ltd 2005.

Quant, Mary. *Quant by Quant*. Cassell & Co Ltd 1966.

Rous, Lady Henrietta (ed) *The Ossie Clark Diaries*. Bloomsbury 1998.

Index

Acknowledgements

Special thanks to Allan Hutchings for his wonderful photography and to Patrick Young of Vintage Modes and Sarah Caverhill at Grays Antique Market. Thanks to Tina Persaud and Verity Muir at Anova books, and Aldo Papaleo of the Ken Scott Archive, Anna Buruma of Liberty of London, Bernard Nevill, Caroline Cox, Celia Birtwell, Fiona Grimer, Glenys Hollingsworth, Natalie Gibson, Jenny Hoon, John Angus, Linda Wood, Malcolm Bird, Marimekko, Merja Vihunen of the Design Museum, Helsinki, Nicole and Phillip de Leon of Alexander Henry Fabrics, the Victoria & Albert Museum and Zandra Rhodes.

Picture Credits